The Story of
CARS

Katie Daynes

Illustrated by
Adam Larkum

Reading Consultant: Alison Kelly
Roehampton University

Contents

Chapter 1

Early ideas

For hundreds of years, people longed for a vehicle that didn't have to be pushed or pulled.

This is hard work!

"We need a cart that goes by itself," they thought.

As early as the 1400s, Italian inventor Leonardo da Vinci drew plans for a vehicle that was driven by clockwork.

Nobody believed it would work and da Vinci never got around to building it anyway.

4

Another Italian made a wind-powered tricycle. But on calm days it was no better than a chair.

People had to wait 400 more years for a vehicle that could really go by itself.

Chapter 2

Steaming ahead

In the 1700s, steam engines were invented. Nicolas-Joseph Cugnot tried using one to power a cart. It worked, but the heavy engine almost slowed him to a halt.

Thirty years later, Richard Trevithick had a different idea. He used a steam engine to pull a wagon along an iron track – and invented the train.

His friend, Sir Goldsworthy Gurney, was very impressed. But he thought a vehicle that worked on roads would be even better.

Gurney designed a steam
passenger coach that didn't need
tracks. On a flat road, it went at
24 km (15 miles) per hour.

Uphill, it went
very slowly…

...and downhill, it almost
ran away.

I can't stop!

As people quickly found out,
steam vehicles were hard to control
and very easy to crash.

9

Chapter 3

The first cars

Gradually, inventors turned away from steam and tried different engines instead. Some were powered by gunpowder...

...but they blew up.

Others used electricity. The first electric carriages were driven by huge batteries. The only problem was – the batteries quickly ran out of power.

They've stopped twice in ten minutes!

Finally, an engine was made that worked using petrol. Designed by Etienne Lenoir and improved by Nicolas Otto, would this engine be able to power a carriage?

Yes! In 1886, German engineer Karl Benz designed and built the first petrol-driven vehicle. It had three wheels, one seat and a small engine at the back. Benz was delighted with his invention.

Then, the first time he drove it in
public, he crashed into a wall.

But his vehicle worked and word
spread. Soon other inventors were
designing petrol-powered, horseless
carriages – or "cars" for short.

Around the same time, another German, Gottlieb Daimler, built a wooden bicycle with an engine. His son Paul bravely took this "motorcycle" on its first ride...

...and came safely home again.

The following year, Daimler tried his engine inside a carriage. The result was the world's first four-wheeled car.

Benz and Daimler kept building cars, but they never drove them very far.

One day, Berta Benz decided to take her husband's latest car for a spin. She and her sons drove 100 km (60 miles) to visit her mother, giving the old lady the shock of her life.

By the 1890s, several companies were making cars. In France, inventors Panhard and Levassor followed Daimler's design, with one major change.

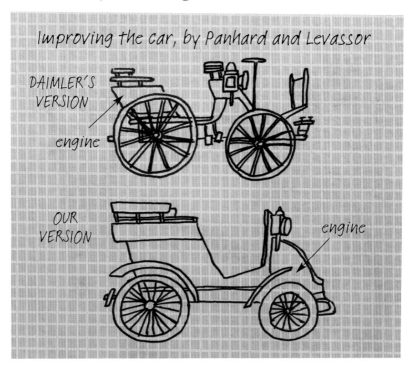

Improving the car, by Panhard and Levassor

DAIMLER'S VERSION

engine

OUR VERSION

engine

After that, most cars had their engines at the front.

Starting a car wasn't easy. First, the driver had to "crank" the engine. This meant turning a stiff handle at the front of the car until a spark managed to fire the engine. On cold days, it took forever.

As the engine spluttered into action, the driver would leap inside and step on the accelerator. This sent more fuel to the engine.

How to start a car:

1. Crank up

2. Jump in

A series of belts and chains connected the engine to the thin, solid wheels. As soon as the driver let the handbrake go, the journey could finally begin.

Turning corners was the next challenge. Drivers had to move a wooden stick, or tiller, to change direction. Luckily, it wasn't long before steering wheels were invented.

Handbrake

3. Release brake

Tiller

4. Go!

Chapter 4

Better designs

Every car company boasted that their designs were best. So, in 1895, they decided to have a race from Paris to Bordeaux – and back again – to show who was right.

Hissss

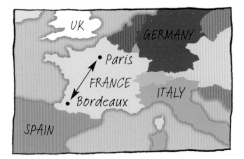

Over 1,130 km (700 miles) and 48 hours later, the race was won by a Panhard-Levassor car.

The Michelin brothers were there too, showing off their new, inflated wheels. They had 22 punctures on the way, but the crowd still thought their tyres were great.

In France, where the race took place, there was no speed limit.

"Why do we have to drive at a snail's pace?" grumbled British drivers. According to the Red Flag Act, a car was only allowed on British roads if someone walked 20 paces ahead of it. Horse owners liked this law. They said horseless carriages scared their horses.

In 1896, the Red Flag Act was finally abolished. At last, British drivers could drive faster than they could walk. Now they needed some exciting new designs.

British engineer, Henry Royce, dreamed of making a really comfortable car. But he was too poor to do it on his own.

Luckily, in 1904, he met Charles Rolls – a rich landowner who loved motoring. With Rolls' money and Royce's skill, the two men went into business.

In 1907, they launched the first great luxury car, the Rolls-Royce *Silver Ghost*.

The *Silver Ghost* was a dream to drive, but not very practical on rough, pot-holed roads.

In America, engineer Ransom Olds took a different approach. He created a car that could cope with bumps and named it the *Oldsmobile*.

With its lightweight frame and strong springs, the *Oldsmobile* was perfect for countryside roads.

But Americans in the city wanted something more snazzy. When the Mercer car company created the *Speedster* and the *Raceabout*, its rich customers were delighted.

Let's overtake that green Raceabout.

Chapter 5

A family car

Early cars were so expensive to make, only a handful of people could afford them. Everyone else just stood and stared as rich motorists roared by.

One day, an American engineer
had a vision. "Wouldn't it be
wonderful if every family had a
car," he thought.

The engineer's name was Henry
Ford and he was determined to
make cars cheaper.

He set up a large factory in America and positioned his workers in a long line. This way, lots of cars could be assembled at the same time.

Since the cars were built from identical parts, they all looked exactly the same.

In 1908, the world's first mass-produced cars rolled off Ford's assembly line. Known as *Model T* Fords, they gave a bouncy ride, but at least they were cheap.

As thousands of people rushed to buy *Model T*s, Ford wanted to build them even faster.

Then doors.

Tyres first.

In 1913, he had a breakthrough –
a moving assembly line. With a
belt carrying the cars from worker
to worker, Ford was soon making
them in record time and selling
them more cheaply still. Owners
grew fond of their new cars, even
giving them a pet name, Tin Lizzie.

Chapter 6

Happy motoring?

Not another nail!

More and more people took to the roads, but the roads weren't ready for them. Nails from horseshoes littered the rough surfaces and punctures were common.

Even worse, with no road signs
drivers didn't know what was
coming next, so lots of cars crashed
or veered into hedgerows.

Yikes!

Road by road, teams of workers
smoothed out the bumps and
covered the surfaces with tar and
gravel. Huge signs were set up
along the way, to warn drivers of
hidden dips and bends.

33

The police wanted traffic signals too. In 1868, a traffic light had been invented to control horse-drawn carriages. Red on one side and green on the other, it seemed like a great idea... until a London policeman tried to turn it around.

BANG!

For the next 50 years, most traffic signals were simply wooden arms on sticks. Arms out meant stop, arms in meant go.

STOP   STOP

GO

34

But drivers were still
confused at junctions.

Crunch!

Stop!

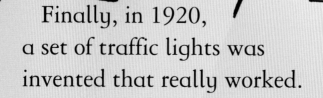

Finally, in 1920,
a set of traffic lights was
invented that really worked.

Over time, roads grew safer and so did cars. In 1903, a new British law said cars must have two lamps at the front and one at the back. Two years later, the car bumper was invented.

Bump!

No harm done!

Cars also became easier to use. Instead of getting arm ache cranking the engine, drivers just had to press a starter switch. And, rather than pulling over because of the rain, most cars now had windscreens with wipers.

You need a new car!

Motoring was great fun, but not everyone was happy. In Britain, there was a new speed limit of 32 km (20 miles) an hour. The police set up traps to catch anyone driving too fast.

Angry drivers grouped together to think up ways of avoiding the traps. They called themselves the Automobile Association, or AA for short.

AA patrolmen were sent on bikes to check where the police had set their speed traps. Then they cycled off to warn AA members.

The speed limit was abolished in 1930, delighting the AA. But then the patrolmen were out of a job.

"Let's offer a breakdown service instead," they decided. And they're still offering it today.

Chapter 7

All kinds of cars

Every year the number of drivers multiplied – and so did their choice of cars. Two popular designs in the 1920s were the little *Austin Seven* and the larger *Bullnose Morris*.

In the 1930s, an Italian company, Fiat, made the world's smallest, mass-produced car. Inside, there was just enough room for two people. But then the nose had to be extended to make room for the engine.

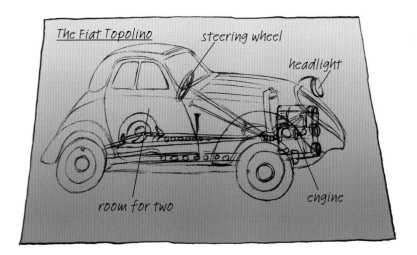

The Fiat Topolino

steering wheel

headlight

room for two

engine

The car looked very cute. People called it *Topolino*, the Italian word for little mouse.

The world's best-selling car was originally the idea of the German dictator, Hitler. In 1933, he ordered Ferdinand Porsche to design a very cheap family car.

Porsche went to Ford's factory in America for inspiration. By 1936, he had come up with a groovy, curvy design.

The car was nicknamed *Beetle* because it looked like one.

In the 1960s, a British design stole the limelight. It was a small box-shaped car with tiny wheels, named the *Morris Mini Minor*, or *Mini* for short. Competitions were held to see how many people could squeeze inside.

There's room for one more!

Europeans loved *Topolinos*, *Beetles* and *Minis*. They were affordable, full of character — and easy to park.

Chapter 8

American giants

Meanwhile, American designers were thinking big. Their cars were getting longer and lower – and guzzling huge amounts of fuel.

Wow! I want a car like that!

In 1947, the *Studebaker Starlight* started a trend for sleek, stylish cars. The following year, a designer working for the Cadillac car company was inspired when a fighter jet flew by.

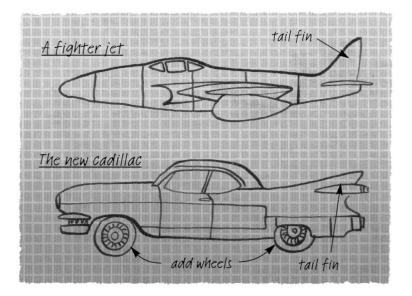

A fighter jet

tail fin

The new cadillac

add wheels

tail fin

American designers used every trick to make their cars stand out, from stylish fins and shiny chrome bumpers to dazzling paintwork and pointed tail-lights.

Dad! Come for a spin in my new car.

Most impressive of all were the stretch limos.

Still popular today, they are twice the length of a normal car, with plush leather seats and a drinks' bar inside.

The rich and famous love to travel by limo. They can soak up the sights in chauffeur-driven luxury, while mirrored windows stop excited fans from seeing in.

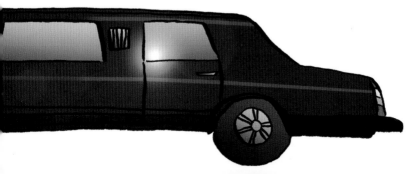

Much cheaper and more practical was the 1960s' station wagon. A huge box on wheels, it made a great family car because there was room for everyone and everything.

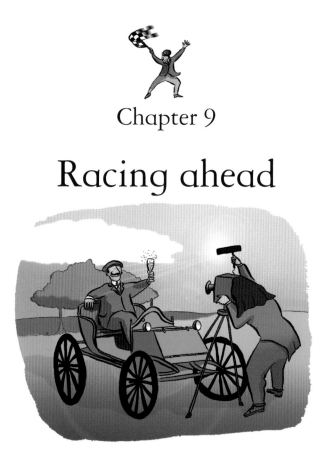

Chapter 9

Racing ahead

Ever since cars were invented, drivers have enjoyed stepping on the accelerator. In 1898, a French Count set the first land speed record of 65 km (40 miles) per hour.

His record was soon broken by an electric car...

...and then, surprisingly enough, by a steam-powered one.

While some drivers chased speed records, others were chasing the car in front. Racing became an exciting new sport and inventors worked hard to design the best racing car.

Maybe a longer car will finish first...

I was inspired by a chunk of cheese!

In 1911, Panhard Levassor built a car for the racing driver, René de Knyff. They made a boat shape from plane materials and added wire-spoked wheels. The result was a stylish, lightweight sports car.

After World War I, a plane engineer named Walter Bentley decided to switch to racing cars – with huge success. At the 24-hour race held in Le Mans every year, his cars won five times.

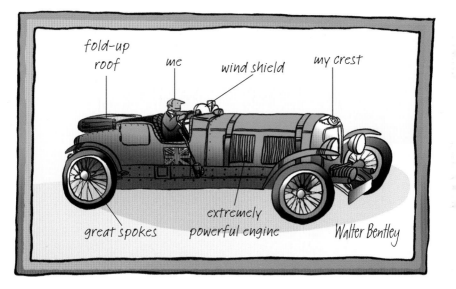

fold-up roof

me

wind shield

my crest

great spokes

extremely powerful engine

Walter Bentley

In the 1927 race, a Bentley car was damaged in a big crash, but still crossed the finish line first.

Over the decades, racing cars became lower, sleeker and *much* faster. By the 1960s, they needed an extra frame at the back to stop them from taking off.

Crowds at race tracks grew bigger each year, especially for the popular Grand Prix races. Everyone wanted the thrill of watching fast cars zoom past.

Meanwhile, the land speed record was soaring higher and higher. Malcolm Campbell, in his bullet-shaped *Bluebird*, was the first to reach 480 km (300 miles) per hour.

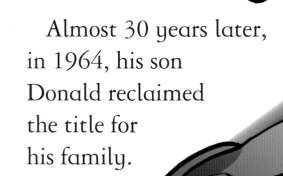

Almost 30 years later, in 1964, his son Donald reclaimed the title for his family.

Donald's car, also named *Bluebird*, hurtled across the Australian desert at 642 km (401 miles) per hour.

But before the end of the year, Art Arfons from America drove his *Green Monster* 55 km (34 miles) faster.

In 1997, British driver Andy Green made his own bid to break the world record in America. As he sped across the Black Rock desert in *Thrust SSC*, his team heard a massive...

(((BOOM!)))

Reaching 1,220 km (760 miles) per hour, Green had driven faster than the speed of sound!

Chapter 10

What next?

Today, there are more cars on the roads than ever. They use up lots of fuel and puff horrible fumes into the air.

Whiff!

Now, engineers are inventing cars that won't pollute the air. They might run on energy from the sun...

...or give off water instead of nasty fumes.

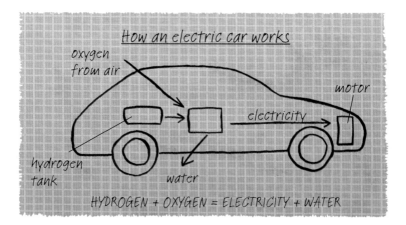

How an electric car works

oxygen from air

motor

electricity

hydrogen tank

water

HYDROGEN + OXYGEN = ELECTRICITY + WATER

Tomorrow's cars will be all kinds of astonishing shapes. Some of them may even fly.

Cars timeline

Da Vinci's design
1400s

Cugnot's tractor
1770

Gurney's steam coach
1827

First electric carriage
1830s

Mercer's Raceabout
1910

Model T Ford
1908

Rolls & Royce's Silver Ghost
1907

René de Knyff's sports car
1911

Bullnose Morris
1912

First Bentley
1919

Green Monster

Donald Campbell's Bluebird
1964

Mini
1960

Volvo Estate
1953

Renault Espace
1984

Porsche Boxster
1996

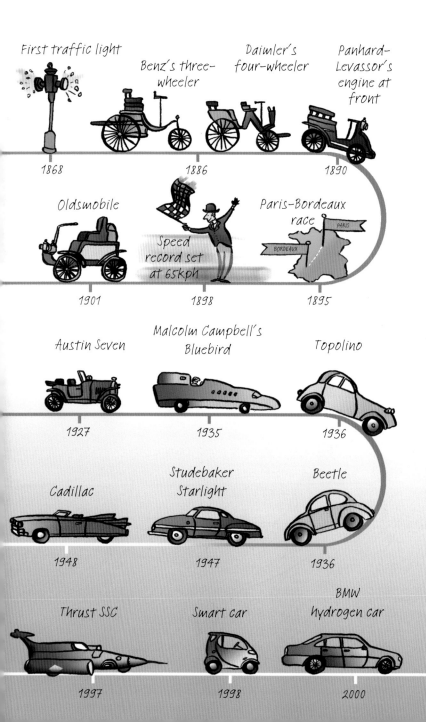

First traffic light

Benz's three-wheeler

Daimler's four-wheeler

Panhard-Levassor's engine at front

1868

1886

1890

Oldsmobile

Speed record set at 65kph

Paris-Bordeaux race

PARIS

BORDEAUX

1901

1898

1895

Austin Seven

Malcolm Campbell's Bluebird

Topolino

1927

1935

1936

Cadillac

Studebaker Starlight

Beetle

1948

1947

1936

Thrust SSC

Smart car

BMW hydrogen car

1997

1998

2000

Historical advice: Gillian Bardsley, Archivist,
British Motor Industry Heritage Trust

Series Editor: Lesley Sims

Designed by Russell Punter
and Doriana Berkovic

Researched by Jane Bingham

This edition first published in 2007 by Usborne Publishing Ltd.,
Usborne House, 83-85 Saffron Hill, London EC1N 8RT, England.
www.usborne.com
Copyright © 2007, 2005 Usborne Publishing Ltd.